DESMOND ARMSTRONG

SoccaBoy 1

Socca Boy, How's That Hockey?

Edited by Shawn Lamb
Color graphics by Robert Lamb
Drawings by D. K. Armstrong

Published by 610Media, Nashville, TN.

Printed in the United States of America.

This book is dedicated to my adult children
and my grandchildren.

We call it Kickball.

Between the ages of 10 and 12, my parents would carry me to my Grandma's house in Northeast D.C. every weekend. There in the safety of that cul-de-sac neighborhood, I would be challenged by the many street games we played, as well as by my sense of belonging. In time I came to appreciate who I was and how God had made me.

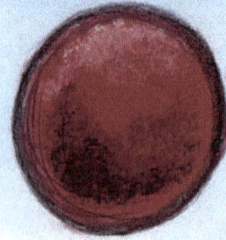

"I declare, Mrs. Joyce, you get prettier by the days. Come here and give me a hug. it's been awhile since I's seen ya," said Mr. Pettis, my Grandma's next door neighbor.

My mother laughing replied as she walked past his fence. "I saw you just last Friday, Mr. Pettis, when I dropped off Jerome."

"That's right. How could I forget?" Mr. Pettis said with an exaggerated surprise, then he turned his attention towards me. "Socca Boy, how's that Hockey going?" he asked.

Without looking I answered, "Fine Sir." My attention was on some of the street games the kids were playing to the sound of Stevie Wonder's latest hit song Living for the City blasting from someone's car stereo.

Each weekend I went to stay with my Grandma. I played any number of street games with the kids that lived in this small neighborhood cul-de-sac of Washington, D.C. There were several games to choose from such as Tag Football, Dodgeball, Hopscotch, Double Dutch, and Slap Boxing. Hopscotch reminded me of frogs hopping from lily pad to lily pad. Slap Boxing looked interesting, 'cept I did see some boys crying as they ran home. But the game I loved to play the most was Kickball.

As we walked through my Grandma's front door, I was welcomed by the familiar smell of fried pork chops, greens and mac & cheese. Grandma's mac & cheese wasn't that Kraft blue box stuff, but the real thing made from scratch.

"Jerome, you are getting bigger by the minute. I know you are here every weekend, but I guess when you turned 12 you just started taking off. Come here and give me a hug," Grandma said.

I tried to say "Hi Grandm—", but my words got swallowed up in her embrace.

My Grandma was a big, warm woman who had an even bigger heart, and always helped her neighbors and community with meals, money and most of all prayer. I loved hugging her because I got lost in her loving arms.

She said, "Let me look at you. Yep, you have grown. You were at my stomach last week and now you're almost at my shoulder."

My mother added, "Mama, I just got him a pair of pants this past weekend that went down past his shoes and today, Friday, they are at his ankles."

"Honey, Lawd knows with him growing like that he needs lots of food," Grandma said while smiling at me.

I went upstairs to drop my overnight bag in the bedroom while Grandma continued on about the cost of raising kids compared to when she reared my moms, her sister and her brother. I wanted to get back outside as quick as I could, because it would be dark soon and time to come back in. Also, dinner would be ready and I'd be hungry for sure. Just as I was about to skip down the stairs and out the door, I heard …

"Soldier, you haven't reported for duty. It's 1800 hrs with visibility soon to fade and you must collect your orders. No one from my command leaves unprepared." It was the Colonel. He served in three wars before being discharged due to health reasons.

Upon hearing his voice I quickly straightened up and answered, "Sir, Yes Sir."

He gave me my assignment by sternly saying, "The enemy has tried to breach our lines by deploying some sort of chemical warfare. I believe it was a stink bomb."

Translation: keep away from the bathroom.

He continued. "The sun is trailing toward the western hemisphere leaving 120 minutes of remaining non-generated light."

Translation: it'll be dark soon.

The Colonel ended with, "The mess hall will be primed with goodies and I hope you don't linger once the mission is over."

Translation: food will be gone if I drag my feet in the street.

After receiving my orders, I headed down the steps, kissed Moms goodbye and hit the pavement. Landing on the other side of my Grandma's fenced yard, I dropped in the middle of a shouting match between Reggie and Darryl.

"I tagged you!" yelled Reggie from the middle of the street. "Right here!" Most considered Reggie the best athlete in the neighborhood because he was a bit older and bigger than most of the kids. He was 14, where the rest of us were around 10, 11 or 12 years old.

"Na Aaah!" protested Darryl. "Touchdown! Game!"

Darryl lived round the corner, down the street. He and Reggie were kind of the same because of their age and also the only time they weren't both on the street was when they were hungry. The difference between them was that Reggie went to his house to eat and Darryl … I don't really know where he went. Can't say anyone really knew where he went. But what I can say is that everyone knew when Darryl showed up so did trouble. He was always arguing about something.

"That ain't game and that ain't no touchdown! I tagged you out!" shouted Reggie.

Again Darryl protested, "Na Aah!"

Reggie insisted, "Ah Huh!"

And it began …

"Na Aah!"
"Ah Huh!"
"Na Aah!"
"Ah Huh!"
"Na Aah!"
"Ah Huh!"

Finally, I suggested that we play Dodgeball, since Tag Football was at a standstill. This way everyone could see who got tagged with the ball. It also gave me a way into the game.

"Good idea Socca Boy. I'll be the thrower and the rest of you have to run from the end zone, where Darryl is, to the other end," Reggie proclaimed.

We all crowded into the street opening where Darryl was standing. I noticed that my Moms was leaving for home to meet up with my Father. "Bye Mom," I said.

She replied, "See you Sunday, Jerome. Love you."

"See you Sunday, Jerome. Love you", mimicked Darryl.

Before I could defend my Moms, Reggie declared, "Go on run, so I's can smack you upside your head with this ball."

We prepared to dash to the other side, without getting hit by Reggie.

Darryl started yelling, "You couldn't tag me with your hand and you can't tag me with that ball!" The other kids joined Darryl in boasting of their ability not to get hit.

The key to "Dodge ball" is to either be fast enough not to get hit or hide behind other people. I chose speed and I took off. Before Reggie could start his next comments of certain doom to us, I arrived at the other end. I watched the others in their attempt to cross over and saw Darryl ducking behind a few bodies as not to get hit. Of course, the kids that he used as shields were the ones that got knocked out. With a series of stops and go's, with balls rebounding off cars, the final two dodgers were me and Darryl.

"I'm gonna win this 'Socca Boy'. You think you're fast enough to leave me behind, but I'm faster than you. They call me shadow," said Darryl.

While moving around to prepare for the take-off I noticed two things. The first being Darryl trying to match my every step and the second, Reggie gritting his teeth from frustration over not having knocked Darryl out yet. With this I took off and suddenly stopped. I knew Darryl would try to stay with me. But now he actually ran past me into open territory and into Reggie's focused gaze. Reggie did not hesitate and—

SWAT!

—cracked Darryl on the side of his face.

"I got you like I said I would!" announced Reggie.

"Darryl, man, you should have seen your face when he hit you. You were like frozen, man," said one kid.

"Yeah, and your face looked like a prune," said another.

Listening to the others getting their verbal jabs a familiar sound started to ring my ears.

Swish!

Swish!

Swish!

Swish!

Swish!

Swish!

...DOUBLE DUTCH.

As they jump, bounce, and turn
I was quick to learn.
That I had not the skill
To create this natural thrill.

Rhythm and Rhyme
Are joined in time
With the flip of the wrists
And the sounds of Swish, Swish.

Doubles in Rope
Don't capture full scope
It's the pair with flair
Synchronized in midair
A sight that's now rare
That causes my despair.

Even though I knew how to jump rope, Double Dutch scared me a little because those ropes moved like helicopter blades and plus I could never remember those rhymes while jumping.

Mostly girls played Double Dutch. It kind of went along the same lines as Patty Cake where rhyming is important. Jumping rope was one thing, especially if you were pretending to be a boxer. But other than that most boys didn't bother with it. We needed something that allowed us to use all of our energy and compete against someone at the same time.

It was time for Kickball!

"Socca Boy! You pick a team and I'll pick a team," said Reggie.

"Awight," I replied. Everyone lined up in the center of the cul-de-sac on the grassy mound and I said, "James!" before Reggie could think.

He called, "Lavar."

I said, "Zaire."

Reggie picked Roc and I called, "Skinny."

"Teisha," declared Reggie.

I selected Remi as my last pick.

By this time Reggie had figured out why, I jumped at going first. Darryl was the very last pick and it was Reggie's turn.

"Daang!" yelled Reggie turning with his team to be up first. "We're the 'Kung-Fu Kickers and we're going to kick-your butts!" yelled Reggie.

I guess he figured since we were using out feet and Kung-Fu was about kicking, it made perfect sense. Plus everyone loved Bruce Lee. I picked the 'Cosmos' for our team name, since I saw them on television.

Zaire said, "Naaaw, Socca Boy, we ain't goin' with no galaxy, stars, universe junk. We're gonna be the *Underdogs*."

This kind of made sense we were younger, smaller and not from the neighborhood. James hailed from Jamaica, Zaire Africa, Skinny lived in C-Black, Remi arrived from El Salvador and I only came on the weekend.

Everyone said …

"Yeah"
   "Yeah"
      "Yeah"

Now that we had a name, picking the bases was next. We selected cars parked around the cul-de-sac. First base was Mr. Pettis' 1964 Chevy Impala, second was ole' Mrs. George's, (Mama G's) yellow station wagon and third was Jojo's 1972 pick-up. For home we always chose the classiest car, Colonel Ford's Cadillac Seville. It also, helped that his car was always parked in the same spot on the street. Everyone knew that if you rounded third and sprinted home it guaranteed a point because the thrower wasn't going to risk missing you and hitting that car.

Colonel Ford absolutely loved his car.

Once—the story goes—some kids were playing four square and one of the kids slammed the ball in the square for the knock out and the ball bounced all the way to the Colonel's car. It hit the hood, rolled up the windshield and bounced over the top of the car onto the trunk.

This happened right after the Colonel had finished washing, drying and waxing his Cadillac Seville by hand. This regimented process took all day and was a source of pride for every big car owner.

So, once the ball rested in the street, Colonel Ford went to the house, collected his service pistol, came back, collected the ball and took it to his backyard. Then there was a loud noise and that ball hasn't been seen since.

From then on no one—I mean NO ONE—messed with The Colonel.

With the bases set the *Kung-Fu Kickers* were up first because I took first pick. As we took our positions a thought came to my mind. How are those two, (Reggie and Darryl,) going to compete together?

I wasn't the only one thinking this because Skinny said, "Man, if those two keep fighting we got this," as he headed to the grassy mound.

James agreed, "All we gotta do is work together."

Teisha was first up and she moved forward.

I said to Reggie and Darryl, who were both pretending to be Bruce Lee, "That looks about right, ya'll be kicking air when Skinny gives the first pitch."

Both Reggie and Darryl said, "Shut-up Socca Boy!"

Reggie followed up with, "G'on, pitch the ball already! Ya'll's gonna get beat."

Then Darryl chimed in with, "Yeah, all ya'll play like a bunch of girls!"

Teisha pushed Darryl out of the way and prepared to kick. "I'll show you".

She was Reggie's younger sister, tough and had on some Buster Browns. Buster Brown was a popular shoe store that almost everyone shopped. If you didn't have a pair of shoes from Buster

Brown then you were like from a different planet.

Skinny gave a firm roll of the ball with no spin and not too much speed. When the ball rolled closer, Teisha's eyes lit up because she knew she could—

SMACK!

Buster Brown had just made perfect contact with a red rubber ball.

The ball lifted over our heads and beyond Skinny's long arms. We all turned to see it drop into Mama G's yard. Teisha was not only tough, she was smart.

Mama G had an old, cranky white mutt called Chowder, and you never knew whether he would let you go or chew your backside up.

The ball had to be retrieved quickly, because Teisha skirted past Mama G's yellow station wagon. We all looked at each other to see who wanted bite marks. We paused for a moment more and Teisha tagged home.

SCORE!

Kung-Fu Kickers-1
Underdogs-0

Man! We were down 1-0, and all you could hear was them hooping and hollering. Not only that, but we didn't have a ball. We all valued our backsides more than that ball.

So, to take the focus off of their team I said, "Yeah, that's right, your best player is Teisha because she is the only one that can get you points."

The laughing stopped and Darryl, said, "I got your best player. ROLL THE BALL!" as he stepped up to kick.

This time Skinny whipped a fast spinning ball to Darryl. He sliced a pop kick straight to Zaire's hands. Out. Score: One run, One out.

Reggie started to complain about Darryl's out to the point that Lavar and Roc jumped in.

"Come on Darryl, how could you miss kick that ball," said Lavar.

"Chump, my little 5-year-old brother could do better than that!" said Roc.

Darryl shot back with, "You should know Roc, because he beats you in Dodgeball, Kickball, Hopscotch, and Slap Boxing."

With his eyebrows scrunched together in the center of his forehead, Roc stepped up to the plate.

Skinny nodded his head and he prepared to roll the ball. Skinny put a special backspin on the ball so that it would come fast but fall short of the plate. It's best used for the overeager kickers. He may have been thinking that Roc might to try and kill the ball to show he was better than his little 5 year old brother. It proved a good guess, as the ball skipped out fast and then slowed right before Roc could make full contact.

The result: Roc kicked it straight back to Skinny without meaning to.

Score:

1 run, 2 outs.

"I'm going next," said Reggie sensing that he'd better do something now or the *Kung-Fu Kickers* would have three straight outs.

Lavar protested, "It's my turn. You can't change the order. That ain't fair. It's my turn, it's my turn, it's my turn!"

Backing down Reggie said, "Okay, okay, okay. You go, but stop crying like a baby about it. I was only trying to shake things up a little."

Lavar was big for 10 years old with long arms and long legs. He reminded me of a newly born horse still figuring out his body.

Skinny gave Lavar the back pocket tricks starting with the spitter. This is when everybody on the team spits on the ball in the same spot, so the kicker would see the ball rolling toward them. They try not to kick that spot as not to get spit on their shoes.

Strike 1.

Next came the bouncer. That's where you skip bounce the ball so that the kicker will miss time the ball and kick air.

Strike 2.

Finally, Skinny selected a change-up called the "slow roll." Realizing that Lavar appeared a bit clumsy, Skinny went from fast to slow hoping for the last strike. By this time the *Kung-Fu Kickers* were feeling the pressure.

Teisha said, "Come on Lavar, even you can't miss that slow rolling ball!"

In mid-swing, in a split second, Lavar paused to say something then decided not to and followed through on the mid-swing and missed the ball.

Strike 3 — OUT!
SCORE:

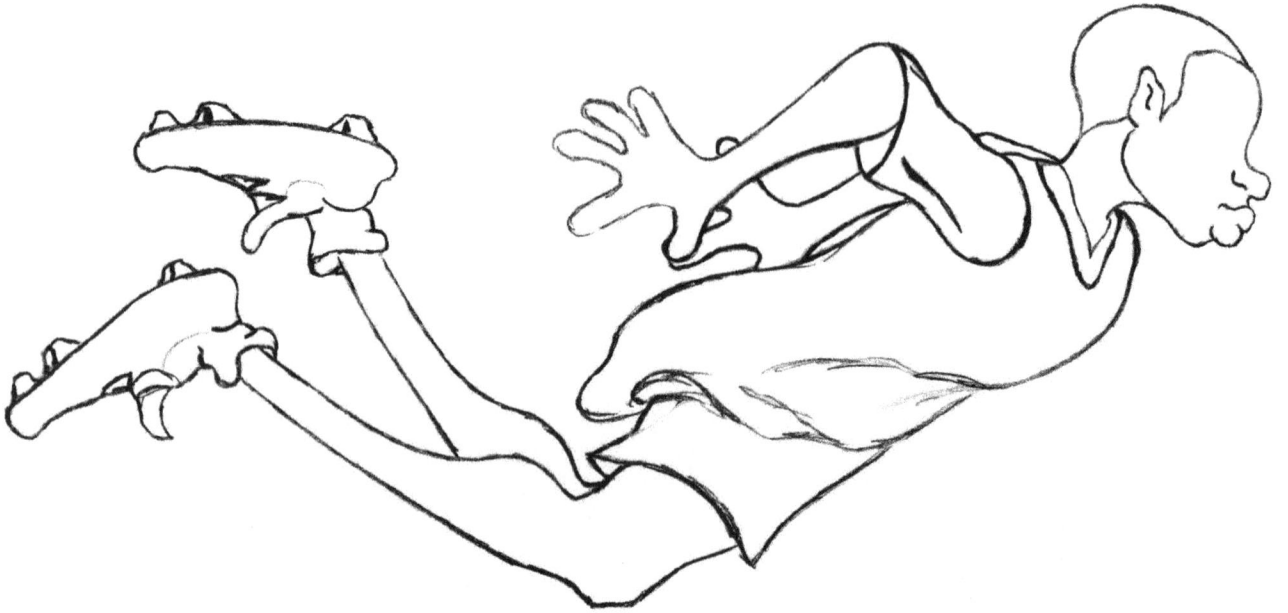

The *Underdogs* up.

Now the cap was off. Lavar yelled at Teisha, Darryl fussed at Roc and Reggie screamed at all of them because he didn't get his chance to kick. While the *Kung-Fu Kickers* tore each other down, we told Skinny how good he did on the mound.

"Great spin balls, Skinny," said James.

Remi added, "Man, I don't think that I could've kicked that 'slow roll' of yours."

I concluded the praise with, "Let's hope that whoever they have is not as good as Skinny."

While we chose who went first, I turned to see who was on the mound. Reggie wasn't smiling when our eyes connected. He looked focued, but the rest of the *Kung-Fu Kickers* kept insulting each other.

Zaire said, "Socca Boy, you go first cause you's always kick'n sump'n."

He was right. Since I started playing soccer, I would kick everything in my path.

Before I stepped up to kick, I reminded myself of the many different kicking selections. There was the chip kick, the side foot kick, the volley kick, the half-volley kick, the scissors kick, the side scissors kick, the front scissors kick, the bicycle kick, and the banana kick. It really didn't matter what kind of spin Reggie put on the ball, because the ball is always moving in a soccer game.

I learned how to play soccer when my family moved further away from the city out to the suburbs. Out there, I remember the kids played something with a rolling round ball with no bases. They asked me if I knew how to play soccer and I said yeah, but we call

it kickball. After running all over an open field for about an hour, I soon realized that soccer was nothing like kickball.

Reggie selected speed as his weapon against me. He rolled two speed balls off to the left and right of the home base before I—

Yeah, I put that ball over their heads and beyond Mama G's yard.

WOPP!

They had to hop two fences in order to pick that ball up from the back alley. I traveled around the bases until I reached home where all the *Underdogs* greeted me.

"Give me five!"
"Give me five!"
"Give me five!"

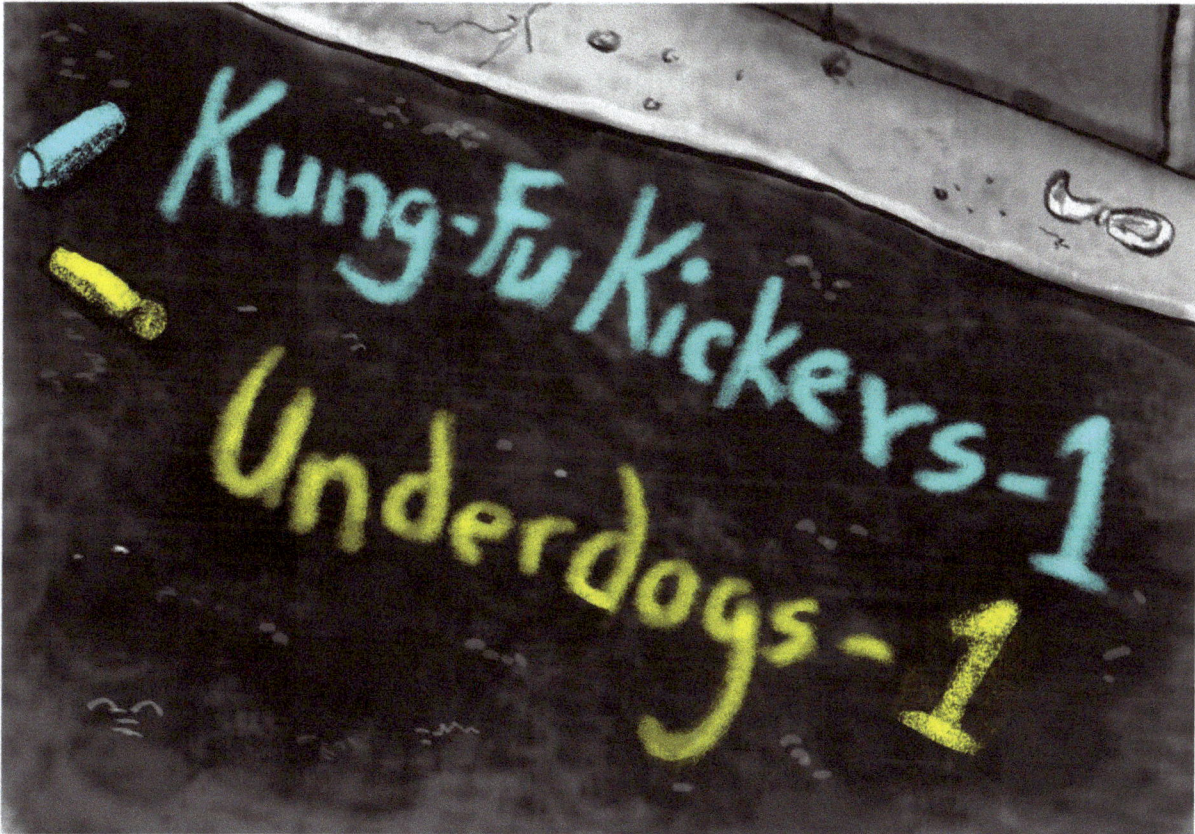

"I ain't got the skills for kick'n a ball like you, Socca Boy, but I do got me a little sump'n for them," said Zaire. And from there, Zaire stood at home base and called out, "Ya'll get ready cause I'm going to wop that ball so far that ya'll be pick'n it up from C-Black."

That was the name of the neighborhood down the street, because everyone that lived in that cul-de-sac had a black car. Someone once said, that everywhere you would look, you would See Black

Still fuming from the last run, I could see Reggie's eyebrows touching each other. He was determined to get Zaire out so that the rest of the *Kung-Fu Kickers* couldn't say anything.

On the first pitch Zaire planted his feet and bent his knees anticipating take off. The ball arrived in quick fashion and Zaire drew back his leg as to take a big swing then he stopped his leg suddenly in order to step on top the ball and stop it. Then Zaire bolted to first base.

Before Reggie or any of the *Kung-Fu Kickers* could react, Zaire headed to second.

Roc, the second baseman, yelled, "Get the ball, man, and throw it here so's I can tag him out!"

Teisha joined in, "Stop standing there looking all dumb and get the ball!"

Zaire flashed past second base when Darryl screamed, "Come on stupid, throw it, throw it, throw it here!"

Moving toward Jojo's 1972 pick up, Reggie clutched the ball, sprinted across the mound and carried an angry gaze in Zaire's direction. He threw the ball with all the motion of a tornado but aimed at Darryl instead of Zaire.

THUMP!

Everyone froze in place when the ball bounced past Jojo's pick up truck. Darryl must have heard ringing in his ears, because he started slapping the side of his head.

Skinny yelled, "Run Zaire, run like the African you are and tag home base!"

We all knew that Zaire was a place in Africa, because Zaire's parents told us this after we wondered, out loud, "Why ya'll wearing those funny looking tablecloths?" Zaire squirted over to Colonel Ford's Cadillac Seville and tagged home base.

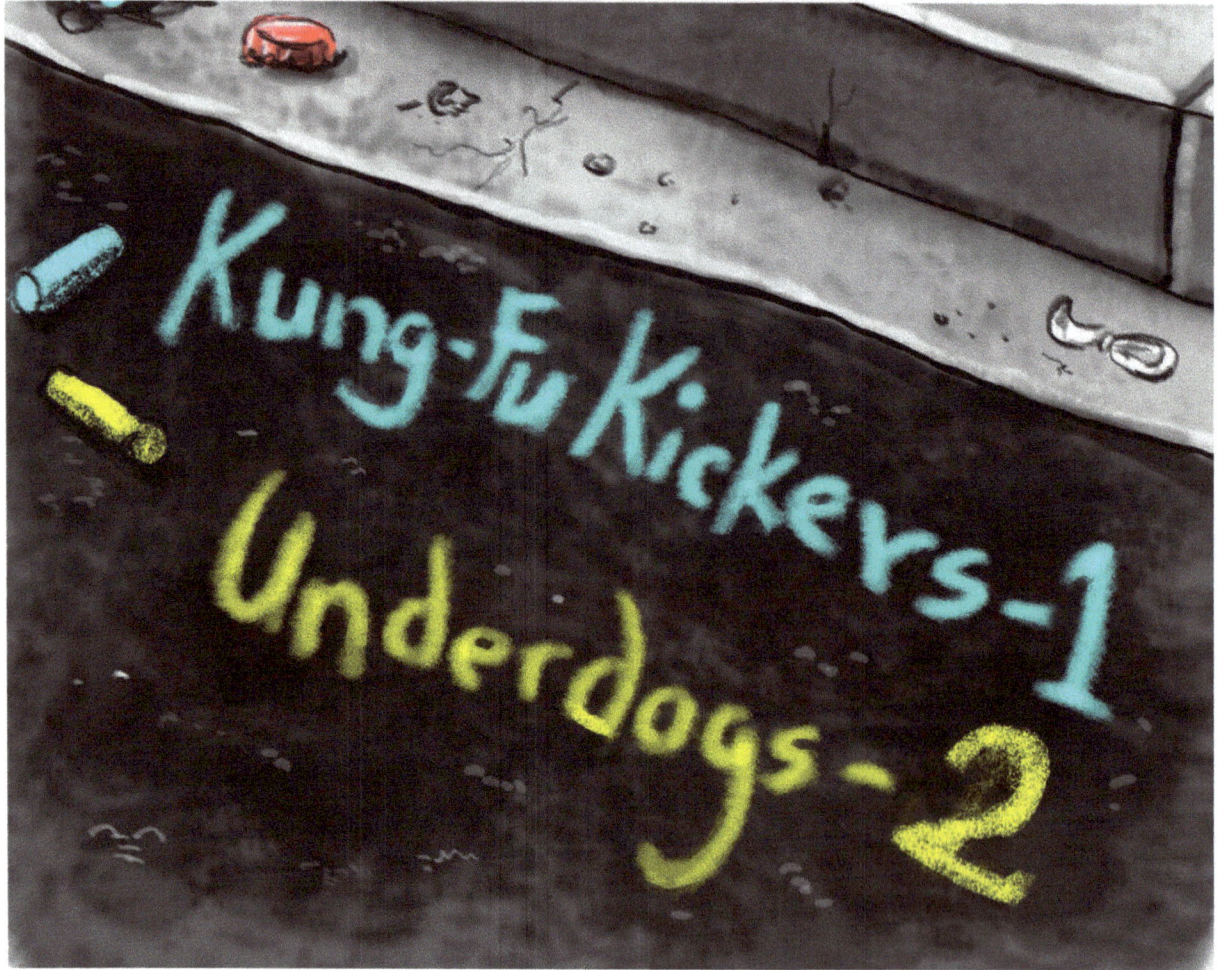

In the distance—I mean from round the corner and down the street—we heard, "Darryl! Darryl! Where are you, Boy?" That signaled the score was 1-2 and we would either continue tomorrow or finish it on the next kick.

"Awight Remi, bring us home," said James, who would be up next if there was enough light. We all had to be off the street when dark.

Remi said, "Hey James, I'll make this one for me and you."

"Mash-it-up, boy!" replied James.

The ball came rolling toward Remi, and saw the ball leaving a mark on the street after it fully rotated. Remi let the pitch go, so that he could figure it out.

Strike 1.

A DUKEY BALL!!!!

It turned out that someone on the *Kung-Fu Kickers* team had wiped the ball in dog poop. It is a certain strikeout, because no one wants dog poop on their shoes.

Remi waited for the next roll with an expression of eagerness on his face. None of us could figure it out.

When the DUKEY BALL came, we heard a splat and saw the ball heading toward Teisha. I guess she was so surprised that Remi kicked the ball that she didn't see it coming her way. It hit her smack in the middle of her stomach and stuck there for what seemed like a week before it dropped to the ground.

Remi tagged bases and headed to home base.

Teisha cried and screamed with her hands in the air as not to touch the dog poop while running. We could still hear her screaming after she slammed the door behind her at her house.

Meanwhile Remi tagged home base and we won the game. Nobody would pick the ball up after Remi kicked it.

After our excitement was silenced by an unwanted odor, I asked, "Why did you kick that ball knowing you would get dog poop all over your shoe Remi?"

He said, "I knows my moms will buy me a new pair of shoes before she would clean dese."

GAME!

The street lights popped on, so I headed to my Grandma's house. "Later."

Reggie responded, "See ya tomorrow".

He lived two doors over from my Grandma's house. Reggie didn't even look at me when he said it. I guess he stilled tried to figure how they lost with everybody they had on the Kung Fu Kickers.

Right when I stepped in the house I heard, "Darryl! Darryl! Where are you, Boy?! in the distance. I turned to look back to the street and caught a glimpse of Darryl scooting around the corner in the direction of his house.

Uumph … What is that sweet smell that's greeting me at the door? Grandma baked her specialty, cream cheese pound cake with strawberries and Cool whip. I was cool with just the fried chicken.

"Soldier, get to the latrine and scrub. Use the one downstairs, as I believe there is still residue from the earlier stink bomb. Better to be safe. The table is set and I'm about to say grace," said the Colonel.

I wasted no time, in and out before the Colonel reached the head of the table. Grandma was just setting the bowl of greens on the table and took her seat.

"Lord, bless this food. Amen" said the Colonel.

"Ford …" Grandma disappointedly said.

So, the Colonel started again. "Lord God, we ask that you bless the hands that have prepared this food and bless this food to the nourishment of our bodies to the glory of your name."

Grandma added, "Father God, remember Darryl tonight." Then we all said, "In Jesus name, amen."

In the middle of passing the food around the table to place our portions on our plates, the Colonel asked, "Did your troops work as a unit relative to the rules of engagement?"

Grandma quickly rephrased with, "How did this week's kickball game go? I heard a lot of yelling out there"

I responded, "That was the Kung-Fu Kickers screaming at each other because Reggie hit Darryl with the ball instead of getting Zaire out and they were losing. They had the better players, but we had the better teamwork. We weren't as old as them, but like you always say Colonel, 'A small unit can conquer an army even if they are considered to be underdogs ' ".

Desmond Armstrong

About the Author

Husband and father of seven, Desmond Armstrong ranks this fact as one of the greatest of his accomplishments. Born at George Washington University Hospital in the nation's capital, Desmond first encountered soccer at the age of eleven. He went on to compete at the collegiate level for the University of Maryland on a soccer scholarship and was drafted to play professional soccer at the conclusion of his college career. After his second year on the pro circuit, he was selected to represent the United States in the Olympics. He also represented the US in the World Cup. Desmond was inducted into the National Soccer Hall of Fame in 2012.

Milton Keynes UK
Ingram Content Group UK Ltd.
UKHW051612021124
450590UK00004B/15

9 781736 282175